# Table of Co I0012683

## 1. Introduction

## 2. Understanding Search Engines

## 3. Keywords

## 4. On-Page SEO

## 8. SEO Analysis and Monitoring

## 9. The Future of SEO

## 10. Conclusion

# 1. Introduction

## 1.1. What is SEO?

Hi there! Since you're here, it's clear that you want to get a perfect understanding of what this whole SEO thing is all about. So, let's not waste any more time and dive right in, so you can become an SEO master as quickly as possible!

What exactly is it? Well, SEO stands for 'Search Engine Optimization'. It sounds pretty technical, right? But don't worry! We're here to break it down into bite-sized, understandable pieces.

Imagine you've baked the world's most delicious chocolate cake. It's there in your kitchen, smelling divine. But here's the catch - if nobody knows about your cake, they can't come to taste it, right?

Think of your website as that delicious cake and SEO as the process of letting people know it exists, guiding them to your kitchen.

SEO is all about improving your website's visibility for relevant searches. The better visibility your pages have in search results, the more likely you are to garner attention and attract prospective and existing customers to your business.

Simply put, SEO is a set of rules for optimizing your website in a way that it achieves higher rankings in search engines' organic results, making it easier for people to find, like they would find your amazing chocolate cake.

In essence, SEO is all about understanding what people are searching for online, the answers they are seeking, the words they're using, and the type of content they wish to consume. Knowing the answers to these questions will allow you to connect to the people who are searching online for the solutions you offer.

Now that you have a basic understanding of what SEO is, let's get ready to dive deeper into this exciting world in the next chapters! It's going to be an exciting journey, so stick around and let's make your website as tempting as that chocolate cake!

## 1.2. Why is SEO Important?

Now that we know what SEO is, let's chat about why it's important. Picture this: you've just set up a beautiful shop in a busy city. You've got dazzling displays, top-quality products, and a friendly team. But there's one problem. Your shop is tucked away in a hidden alley that nobody knows about. How many customers do you think you'll get? Not many, right?

That's where SEO comes into play. It's like a big, flashing neon sign that says, "Hey! We're over here! Come check us out!" SEO helps your website (or your online 'shop') get found by people who are looking for exactly what you've got to offer.

Search engines, like Google, Bing or Yahoo, are the main source of traffic for most websites. They use complex algorithms to understand and rank pages appropriately in search results. But here's the thing: even though these search engines are smart, they still need some guidance.

Optimizing your site will provide the search engines with that guidance, helping them understand what your content is about. This, in turn, improves your chances of ranking higher in search results. And the higher you rank, the more visible your website is, and the more traffic, customers, and revenue you're likely to gain.

But SEO isn't just about search engines. Good SEO practices also lead to a better user experience and usability of a website. It's about creating a smooth, fast, and user-friendly website that provides value to its visitors.

In today's competitive market, SEO is more important than ever. If you want your business to be found online, you have to care about SEO. It's like the breadcrumbs that lead Hansel and Gretel to the gingerbread house, only in our story, the breadcrumbs are leading your customers straight to your online shop.

In the upcoming chapters, we will unpack how to make your website more attractive to both search engines and your human visitors. Get ready for an adventure into the world of SEO!

## Let's test yourself!

**1. If SEO was a plant, what would it be?**

A) A fast-growing weed

B) A delicate orchid

C) A slow-growing oak tree

D) A cactus

**2. What is the main goal of SEO?**

A) To decorate your website with pretty colors and images

B) To make your website visible to as many people as possible

C) To ensure your website has the most pages on the internet

D) To win a popularity contest

### 3. Why is SEO important for a business's digital presence?

A) It guarantees immediate increases in sales

B) It makes sure everyone likes your website

C) It improves the visibility and credibility of your website

D) It allows you to ignore other aspects of your business

### 4. What role does SEO play in a website's ranking on search engines?

A) It's not really important; social media is the key

B) It automatically puts your website at the top of every search

C) It's only relevant for websites that are selling products

D) It helps search engines understand the context of your content

**5. What's one key aspect of SEO?**

A) Inserting as many keywords as possible into your content

B) Sending emails to everyone you know asking them to visit your website

C) Making your website look attractive

D) Creating high-quality content that's valuable to your audience

Remember, good SEO practices are about quality, not quantity, and they're a long-term commitment!

Now check your answers at the end of the book!

## 2. Understanding Search Engines

### 2.1. How Do Search Engines Work?

Let's take a little journey into the heart of a search engine. You've probably used one like Google or Bing countless times, but have you ever wondered how they manage to find exactly what you're looking for in a split second? Well, it's all down to three main steps: Crawling, Indexing, and Ranking. Let's break it down.

**1. Crawling:**

So imagine the internet as a vast city and the search engines as explorers. The explorers start their journey by sending out scouts, known as 'crawlers' or 'spiders' (don't worry, these spiders are friendly!). These digital critters have a single mission: to roam the city, popping into every building (webpage) they can find and checking out what's inside.

They look at everything from text and images to videos and the underlying code that holds it all together. They're thorough, and they don't miss a thing. They even use the city's transport links (or the links on a webpage) to move around.

## 2. Indexing:

After the crawlers have toured the city and noted everything down, they head back home and report their findings. This information is then stored in a gigantic digital library known as the 'index'.

Think of the index as the search engine's personal encyclopedia of the internet. It's where they store a copy of every building (webpage) they've visited. However, not every building makes it to the index. Some might be too run-down (poor quality content), while others might be breaking the city's rules (search engine guidelines).


## 3. Ranking:

Now, when you type a search into Google, what you're really doing is asking the search engine to sift through its vast encyclopedia and find the most relevant entries for you. The search engine ranks these entries in what it believes to be the order of relevance and usefulness, and presents them to you as search results.

The search engine wants to give you the best possible answer to your query, and so it uses a secret recipe (algorithm) to decide the order of the results. The recipe takes into account hundreds of ingredients (ranking factors), some of which we'll be revealing in the next few chapters.

In a nutshell, search engines are like tireless explorers, constantly journeying through the web, making notes, and providing you with the best possible answers to your questions. Understanding how they do this is the first step to making your website more appealing to them (and to your visitors). Stick around, because we're just getting started on this SEO adventure!

## 2.2. Search Engine Algorithms: What You Need to Know

Alright, it's time to talk about something that might sound a bit intimidating at first - search engine algorithms. But don't worry! We're going to break it down and make it as friendly as possible.

So, what's a search engine algorithm? Well, imagine you're at a party with hundreds of people, and you're looking for your friend, Sam. How would you find him? You'd probably start by asking some questions, right? What does he look like? What's he wearing? Who is he likely to be talking to?

Search engine algorithms do something similar. When someone types in a search query, the search engine wants to find the most relevant and useful information to show them, just like you want to find Sam at the party. To do this, it asks its own set of questions about every website it knows. These questions might include:

- How relevant is this website to the search query?

- How popular is this website?

- How authoritative and trustworthy is it?

The way the search engine asks and weighs these questions is its algorithm.

Now, search engine algorithms are not static. They're like chameleons, constantly changing and adapting to give users the best possible results. Google, for example, is known to make thousands of changes to its algorithm each year! That's why SEO is not a 'set it and forget it' kind of thing. It requires continuous learning and adaptation.

So, how can we possibly keep up with these ever-changing algorithms? The good news is, you don't have to understand every tiny detail. Phew! The most important thing to remember is this: search engines aim to provide the best possible results for their users.

That means if you focus on creating high-quality, relevant content and providing a good user experience, you're already on the right track. Search engines will recognize and reward your efforts.

In the next chapters, we'll dive deeper into how you can optimize your website to align with these algorithmic principles. So, let's keep this SEO party going!

## 2.3. The Role of SEO in Digital Marketing

This time, we're going to dive into the role of SEO in the grand scheme of things, namely, digital marketing.

So, picture digital marketing as a big, bustling city. There are tons of different neighborhoods, each with its own vibe and charm. You've got the Social Media district, with its trendy cafes and non-stop chatter. The Email Marketing area is like a reliable old friend, always there with a comforting routine. Pay-Per-Click (PPC) is the flashy, fast-paced downtown with neon lights and big crowds. And then, there's the SEO neighborhood, a key part of town that connects all the others.

SEO is like the infrastructure of our digital marketing city. It's the roads and highways that get people from point A to point B. Without it, the city wouldn't function properly. It helps guide visitors (aka potential customers) to the right destinations (your awesome website), and makes sure they have a smooth and enjoyable journey along the way.

What's more, SEO is like a city planner, always considering the long-term growth and development of the city. While some marketing strategies might give you quick wins, SEO is all about sustainable success. It's a long game, but boy, is it worth it!

With effective SEO, your website can rank higher in search engine results, making it easier for people to find you. It can increase your visibility and credibility, drive more traffic to your site, and ultimately, boost sales and growth.

Sounds pretty awesome, right? But the best part is, SEO and the other digital marketing strategies are not mutually exclusive. They can, and should, work together in harmony. For example, the keywords you use for SEO can also be used in your PPC campaigns or social media posts to create a cohesive brand message.

So, in our digital marketing city, SEO isn't just a neighborhood. It's the framework that holds everything together. It's the master plan for success. And that, my friend, is why SEO is such a big deal in digital marketing. Let's continue our journey and discover more about this fascinating world!

# Let's test yourself!

**1. If search engines were a supermarket, what would the algorithms be?**

a) The shopping cart.

b) The grumpy security guard.

c) The ultra-efficient store manager organizing all the aisles and products.

d) The free samples stand.

**2. What's the best way to charm the mystical creatures known as search engine algorithms?**

a) Write them a heartfelt love letter.

b) Build a quality website with relevant content, optimized keywords, and quality backlinks.

c) Send them a box of digital donuts.

d) All of the above (wishful thinking, we know).

**3. How do search engines see websites?**

a) Through rose-colored glasses.

b) As a delicious multi-layered digital cake.

c) Through crawlers (also known as spiders or bots).

d) They actually prefer audiobooks.


## 4. How does SEO fit into the grand scheme of digital marketing?

a) It's like the salsa to your nachos, bringing flavor and zing to your online presence.

b) It's a whole separate world, like Narnia.

c) It's an essential tool for increasing your website's visibility and driving organic traffic.

d) It's that cousin who shows up uninvited to all family events.


## 5. What's the golden rule of SEO in digital marketing?

a) Always wear a helmet.

b) Content is King.

c) When in doubt, dance it out.

d) There's no such thing as too much glitter.


Hey, don't forget to check your answers at the end of the book!

# 3. Keywords

## 3.1. What are Keywords?

The Secret Ingredients in the SEO Recipe!

So, you might be asking, "What on earth are keywords?" Well, let me tell you, they're much simpler than you might think. Picture this: you're looking for a new recipe for chocolate chip cookies.

You probably won't type into Google, "How do I make a sweet circular dessert with little bits of chocolate inside?" No, you'd probably search for "chocolate chip cookie recipe." And there you have it, "chocolate chip cookie recipe" is your keyword!

In the vast world of SEO, keywords are the words or phrases that people type into search engines. They're the questions people are asking, the services they're looking for, and the products they want to buy. And your job, as an SEO magician, is to make sure your website answers these queries and appears when these keywords are searched. Easy peasy, right?

But remember, it's not just about throwing as many keywords as you can onto your webpage and hoping for the best. No, no, no. Search engines are smart (remember our talk about algorithms?), and they value high-quality, relevant content. So, your keywords need to be used naturally within your content, providing value and answering the questions your potential visitors are asking.

So, to sum it all up, keywords are the magic words that connect searchers with your site. Choose them wisely, use them effectively, and watch as your site climbs the search engine rankings!

## 3.2. How to Find the Right Keywords?

Welcome back, my fellow SEO adventurers! Now that we know what keywords are, it's time to embark on a thrilling treasure hunt – the quest for the perfect keywords. So, grab your virtual shovels and let's get digging!

So, how do we find these golden nuggets of SEO? Well, it's not as tricky as it might seem. Picture yourself as a detective, trying to get into the minds of the people who are searching for the product, service, or information that you're providing. What words or phrases would they type into the search engine? This is your starting point.

But, as any good detective knows, you can't just rely on your gut instinct. No, you need solid evidence. And that's where keyword research tools come in handy. These fantastic tools, like **Google Keyword Planner,**

**Ahrefs** or **SEMrush**, can show you exactly what people are searching for, how often, and how much competition there is for each keyword. It's like having your very own crystal ball!

Remember, the best keywords aren't always the most searched for. They're the ones that are most relevant to your content and have the right balance of search volume and competition. So, don't be tempted by the shiny allure of high-volume keywords if they're not a good fit for your site.

One more tip before we wrap up: don't forget about long-tail keywords. These are longer, more specific phrases that people might search for. They usually have lower search volumes, but they also have less competition and often lead to higher conversion rates. So, they can be real hidden gems!

**Short-tail keywords**

- typically one to two words and are very general. For example:

1. "Running shoes"

2. "Pizza"

3. "Laptop"

4. "iPhone"

5. "Coffee"

These keywords tend to have very high search volumes, but they're also very competitive and not very specific, which can make it harder to rank for them and harder to attract the right audience.

**Long-tail keywords**

- They're longer phrases that are more specific. They tend to have lower search volumes, but they're also less competitive and more targeted, which can make them more effective for SEO. Here are a few examples:

1. "Best running shoes for marathon training"

2. "Gluten free pizza delivery in Chicago"

3. "Laptop with best battery life"

4. "Refurbished iPhone 11 Pro Max"

5. "Organic fair trade coffee beans"

By using long-tail keywords, you can target a more specific audience that's more likely to be interested in what you're offering.

## 3.3. Keyword Research Tools

So, my friend, you now know what keywords are and how to find the right ones. But you're probably thinking, "Surely, there must be some magical tools to help me with this?" Well, you're in luck! There are some fantastic keyword research tools out there to help you uncover those hidden keyword gems. Let's get to know some of them!

1. **Google Keyword Planner**: It's like the Hogwarts of keyword research tools! Google Keyword Planner is a free tool, and it's all about showing you what people are looking for on Google. It gives you ideas for new keywords, shows how often keywords are searched, and even suggests the level of competition you might face for each keyword.

2. **SEMrush**: SEMrush is like a Swiss Army Knife for SEO. This tool can give you detailed data about keyword search volumes, competition, and more. Plus, it can show you what keywords your competitors are using. It's like having your own personal SEO spy!

3. **Moz Keyword Explorer**: Moz's tool is another fantastic assistant in your keyword research journey. It gives you keyword suggestions, SERP (Search Engine Results Page) analysis, and a keyword's search volume. It's like having a crystal ball that can predict your SEO future!

4. **Ubersuggest**: Ubersuggest is like the genie of keyword research tools. It generates long-tail keyword ideas for any topic and shows you the top-ranking SERPs for them.

5. **AnswerThePublic**: This tool is like your personal mind reader, showing you what questions people are asking around your keyword. It's a great way to find long-tail keywords and come up with content ideas that directly answer your audience's questions.

6. **Ahrefs**: Ahrefs is like your friendly neighborhood detective, always ready to dig up useful insights about your website's SEO performance and your competitors. It's your go-to buddy for uncovering the best keywords, checking out backlinks, and essentially helping you become the star of search engine results.

Remember, each of these tools has its own strengths and weaknesses, so it's worth trying out a few to see which one fits your needs best. It's like trying on shoes – you've got to find the one that fits just right!

Let's take the example of an online shop selling toys for dogs. By using a combination of short and long tail keywords, such as 'dog toys', 'interactive toys for dogs', and 'squeaky toys for small dogs', the shop can attract more potential customers and increase their chances of making sales!

1. **Short tail keywords:** dog toys, pet toys, puppy toys, toys for dogs

   ("For" is a preposition and is not usually included as a keyword in SEO. Therefore, "toys for dog" would be considered a short tail keyword since it consists of only two words)

2. **Long tail keywords**: chew toys for puppies, squeaky toys for small dogs, plush toys for large dogs, tough toys for aggressive chewers

3. **Branded keywords:** Kong dog toys, Nylabone dog toys, Chuckit! dog toys

4. **Geographic keywords:** dog toys UK, pet toys USA, puppy toys Canada

5. **Action-oriented keywords:** buy dog toys online, order pet toys, shop for puppy toys

6. **Industry-related keywords:** best dog toys, eco-friendly pet toys, durable puppy toys

7. **Related terms:** dog treats, dog beds, dog collars, dog grooming tools.

During keyword research for your website, remember that you're unlikely to have them all, at least not initially – unless your industry is extremely niche. Focus on quality rather than quantity. Prioritize the most valuable keywords first and create a long-term strategy, such as blogging, for the rest.

Aim for long-tail keywords. Choosing only short-tail keywords as a new website, you won't be able to outrank established sites that have built their positions over many years. Keep in mind that Google is smart and understands variations and inflections. The plural form or inflected cases of your keyword are not entirely new keywords to Google!

I hope you're enjoying our journey into the world of SEO as much as I am. Next up, we'll dive into how to use these keywords effectively. Stay tuned, my SEO apprentice!

## Let's test yourself!

1. **What are keywords in the world of digital marketing?**

   a) Magic words that open secret internet doors

   b) The words you scream at your computer when it freezes

   c) The specific terms people use in search engines to find what they need

   d) The words you type into a search engine to get lost in the internet

2. **Why is it important to find the right keywords for your website?**

a) To make your website look pretty

b) To make sure people can find your website when they're searching online

c) To confuse search engines and make them work harder

d) Because the internet told you to

3. **Which of these is NOT a keyword research tool?**

a) Google Keyword Planner

b) SEMRush

c) Microsoft Excel

d) Ahrefs

4. **Which of these is not a good way to find the right keywords?**

a) Throwing a dart at a dictionary

b) Using Google's "People also ask" feature

c) Researching what keywords your competitors are using

d) Analyzing the keywords that bring traffic to your own site

**5. What should you do after identifying your target keywords?**

a) Add them to your website as much as possible, even if it makes the text unreadable

b) Forget about them and hope for the best

c) Use them strategically in your content and monitor their performance

d) There is no need to identify keywords

Hey, don't forget to check your answers at the end of the book!

# 4. On-Page SEO

## 4.1. URL Structure

The Street Address of Your Webpage

Hey there, SEO superstar! Ready to dive into the exciting world of URL structures? Great! Now, just as you wouldn't want your house address to be a confusing mess, the same goes for your webpage – it needs a clear, easy-to-understand URL structure.

URL, or Uniform Resource Locator, is just a fancy way of saying "web address." It's the specific set of directions that points the internet to the exact page it needs to find on your website. Think of it like the GPS coordinates for every page of your site.

Now, you might be wondering, "Why does my URL structure matter?" Well, just like a neat and tidy street is easier to navigate, a well-structured URL makes it easier for search engines like Google to find and understand your webpages. This can give you a leg up in SEO rankings, and who doesn't want that?

A good URL structure should be logically organized and easily readable, both for the search engines and for humans. That means avoiding long strings of numbers and gibberish. Instead, aim for short, descriptive, and keyword-rich URLs. For instance:

www.mywebsite.com/best-chocolate-cake-recipe is much more appealing and informative than

www.mywebsite.com/post12345, right?

And remember, just as you wouldn't change your home address every other day, try to avoid changing your URLs too often. This can lead to broken links, and trust me, search engines don't like that. Plus, it can confuse your regular visitors.

In the next sections, we'll dive deeper into how you can optimize your URL structure to create a tidy, navigable website that both search engines and your visitors will appreciate. Stay tuned, because we're just getting started on this exciting journey to SEO mastery!

## 4.2. Meta Tags

The Invisible Heroes of SEO

Imagine going to a bookstore (yes, those still exist!). Before you commit to a book, you glance at the cover, maybe read the summary on the back, or even sneak a peek at the first page. Well, meta tags do a similar job for your webpage. They provide search engines and users a sneak peek of what your page is all about without having to dive deep into your content.

"Wait, but I can't see them!" you might say. You're right! Meta tags are like invisible stagehands in a play, doing all the hard work behind the scenes. They exist in the HTML of your webpage and communicate vital info about your page to search engine bots.

There are different types of meta tags, but the two big ones you should know about are the meta title and the meta description.

The **meta title** is the title of your page that shows up in search engine results. It's like the headline of a newspaper article – make it catchy and relevant to the content of the page (50-60 characters). It's a good idea to write the words in the title in capital letters to make them more visible to the user's eyes!

The **meta description** is a brief summary that appears under the title in search results. It's like the blurb on the back of a book – it should be compelling and give a quick overview of what the visitor can expect to find on your page (120-155 characters).

When crafting your meta tags, remember to include your targeted keywords naturally - but no keyword stuffing! We want to play nice with search engines and users alike.

# A good example:

**Keyword:** "most popular dog toys"

**Meta Title:** Top 10 Most Popular Dog Toys of 2023 | Pawsitively Happy

**Meta Description:** Uncover the most popular dog toys that have our furry friends wagging their tails in 2023! From durable chew toys to interactive puzzles. Check it out!

Remember, a good meta title and description should not only include the keyword but also be enticing to potential readers, giving them a good reason to click on your link in the search results.

It's a good idea to add CTA (Call To Action) in your meta description – most often it is added at the end: Check it out! / Click and read our article! / Buy now 50% off! / Watch our video today! / See now!

## 4.3. Content Optimization

Making Your Words Shine on the Web Stage!

Hey there, SEO explorer! You're back for more, and we couldn't be more thrilled. Today, we're stepping into the heart of SEO: Content Optimization. If you've ever wondered how to make your content dazzle in the bright lights of the internet, you're in the right place!

Content Optimization is all about making your website's content as appealing and useful as possible – not just for your readers, but also for those hardworking search engine bots who are always on the hunt for top-notch content.

So, how do you optimize your content? Imagine you're baking a cake. You'd want to use the best ingredients, right? Well, in this case, your ingredients are your keywords. Sprinkle them throughout your content but be careful not to overdo it. Your text should still sound natural and engaging. No one likes a keyword-stuffed, unreadable cake - I mean, content!

Next, think about the structure of your content. Break up large chunks of text into smaller, bite-sized pieces. Use headings and subheadings (remember to include those keywords!) to make your content easy to navigate. It's like cutting your cake into neat, inviting slices.

Don't forget about images and videos too! They add flavor and variety to your content. Just remember to optimize them as well, using alt tags (little descriptions that tell search engines what the image or video is about). It's like adding a label to your cake so everyone knows what deliciousness to expect.

There's no hard and fast rule for the number of images in an SEO article. It depends on the length of the content and the topic. Some posts might be fine with just one or two images, while others, especially longer or more complex posts, might benefit from more visual aids. What's important is that each image adds value to the content, is properly optimized with alt text for SEO, and does not slow down your page loading speed.

Finally, make sure your content is fresh and up-to-date. Regularly updating your content is like always having a fresh cake ready for your guests. Search engines love fresh content, and so do your visitors!

Remember, at the heart of content optimization is the aim to provide value to your readers. When your readers are happy, search engines are happy too.

Remember! The length of the content can vary widely, but a common recommendation is **at least 300 words** for a basic blog post or article. However, in-depth articles, guides, or resources that aim to cover a topic comprehensively might be much longer, even up to 2000 words or more. It's crucial to provide in-depth, valuable information and not just add fluff to reach a certain word count.

# Grab a cheat sheet!

1. **Choose Your Star:** Identify the main keyword for your content. This keyword should be the star of your show, reflecting the main topic of your content.

2. **Set the Stage:** Include your keyword in your headline, making sure it's catchy and relevant. This is your first chance to capture your audience's attention, so make it count!

3. **Make a Grand Entrance:** Try to use your keyword in the first 100-150 words of your content. This helps both your readers and search engine bots understand what your content is about right from the get-go.

4. **Perform Naturally:** Use your keywords naturally throughout your content. Remember to also use synonyms of your keyword. A good rule of thumb is to aim for a keyword density of about 1-2%. That means your keyword should appear roughly 5-10 times in a 500-word article. But remember, don't overdo it – the text should still read naturally!

5. **Break a Leg:** Break up your content (at least 300 words!) into digestible chunks with headings

and subheadings. Bonus points if you can naturally include your keyword in some of these!

6. **Add Some Drama:** Include relevant images or videos to enhance your content . Don't forget to use keyword-rich alt tags to describe them!

7. **Keep the Show Running:** Regularly update your content to keep it fresh and relevant. Search engines and your audience love new material.

8. **Take a Bow:** End with a strong conclusion that summarizes your content. If possible, try to include your keyword here too (last 100 words), but only if it fits naturally.

9. **Connect the Dots:** Incorporate internal and external links in your content to provide additional value to your readers. For internal links, guide your readers to other relevant content on your site. For external links, point them towards authoritative sources that support or expand upon your points. Remember, the anchor text of your links should be descriptive and relevant to the linked content. If it fits naturally, you can even use your keyword in the anchor text. But most importantly, every link should offer something valuable to your reader. It's all about creating a web of information that your reader will find helpful and engaging.

To fulfill all these rules, brilliant WordPress plugins such as 'Yoast SEO' or 'All in One SEO' will assist you. But remember – SEO is an art, not an exact science. These steps are guidelines, not strict rules. The most important thing is to create valuable, engaging content for your audience. Happy optimizing!

## Example of a good written content (in this case – article) on your website:

**Main keyword**: "safe toys for dogs"

**URL:** www.pawsitivelyhappyshop.com/blog/safe-toys-for-dogs

**Meta Title:** Top 10 Safe Toys for Dogs | Pawsitively Happy – Dog Shop

**Meta Description:** Discover the top 10 safe toys for dogs to ensure fun and injury-free playtime. Your furry friend's safety is our priority. Click here and check it now!

**Blog Post:**

**Headline:** Unleashing Fun: The 10 Best Safe Toys for Dogs

If you're on a hunt for safe toys for dogs, you've come to the right place. When it comes to our furry friends, safety is paramount – especially during playtime. We've dug up (pun intended!) the top 10 toys that are not just fun, but safe for your beloved pooch.

If you're a new dog owner and still figuring out the basics, you might find our 'Dog Care 101'[linked to page with "Dog Care 101" to buy/download the guide] guide helpful. It covers everything from feeding schedules to grooming tips, helping you ensure your furry friend stays happy and healthy.

Choosing dog-friendly toys [keyword synonym] for your beloved pet not only provides them with hours of entertainment but also ensures their safety and wellbeing.

*Image: A dog playing with a toy - Alt Tag: Happy dog playing with a safe chew toy*

## 1. The Indestructibone - A gem among safe toys for dogs!

This toy is a favorite among tough chewers. Made from ultra-durable material, the Indestructibone provides hours of chewing fun without the risk of splintering.

*Image: Indestructibone toy - Alt Tag: Durable Indestructibone dog toy*

## 2. The Kong Classic

The Kong Classic is a versatile, safe toy for dogs that can be stuffed with treats to keep your pup mentally stimulated and satisfied.

*Image: Kong Classic dog toy - Alt Tag: Kong Classic, a safe treat-stuffed toy for dogs*

[continue with the other toys...]

While all the toys we've listed are great options, it's important to remember that no toy is truly indestructible. The American Kennel Club [linked to the relevant page on the AKC's website] has a great resource on dog toy safety and what to watch out for.

In conclusion, when choosing toys for your dog, always prioritize safety. The toys listed above are not only entertaining but are also designed with your pup's safety in mind. Remember, a safe dog is a happy dog!

*Image: A bulldog with a pile of toys - Alt Tag: Happy bulldog surrounded by safe toys for dogs*

And there you have it – our top 10 safe toys for dogs. Now, you're all set to make playtime safer and more fun for your furry friend!

## 4.4. Use of Keywords

In this chapter we will talk about the correct use of keywords. It is true that we have already talked about it in several chapters, but here we will gather everything again and repeat.

Think of keywords as the secret sauce in your SEO stew. They add that extra zing that helps search engines, like Google, understand what your content is all about. Ready to stir things up? Let's get cooking!

### What's a Keyword Anyway?

In the simplest terms, a keyword is a word or phrase that people type into search engines when they're looking for information. For example, if you're trying to figure out why your cat is staring at you intently (are you about to be ambushed?), you might type "why does my cat stare at me" into Google. That's your keyword!

### Using Keywords Effectively

The trick with keywords isn't just to sprinkle them willy-nilly throughout your content. Like a master chef, you want to use them strategically. Here are a few tips to guide you:

1. **Title Tag:** Use your keyword in your title tag. This is the headline that shows up in search engine results. It's the first thing people (and search engines) see, so make it count!

2. **Meta Description:** This is the short summary that appears under the title tag in search engine results. Including your keyword here can help search engines understand your content, and it can also help attract readers.

3. **URL:** If possible, include your keyword in your URL. It's another place search engines look to understand what your page is about.

4. **Headings and Subheadings:** Including your keyword in at least one heading and subheading can be beneficial. It helps break up your content and makes it easier for readers (and search engines) to understand.

5. **In the Content:** Use your keyword naturally throughout your content. Remember, the goal isn't to stuff your content with keywords. Instead, aim for a natural flow that makes sense to your readers.

**Long-Tail Keywords**

Here's a little insider tip for you: don't forget about long-tail keywords! These are longer, more specific phrases that people might search for. For example, instead of "dog toys," a long-tail keyword might be "most popular dog toys for large breeds." Long-tail keywords can be less competitive and can help you reach a more targeted audience.

## The Importance of Keywords

You might be wondering, "Why are keywords so important in SEO?" Well, consider this: when you're hungry for pizza, you don't just search for "food," right? You search for "best pizza near me" or "pepperoni pizza recipe." The words you use are the keywords, the guideposts that lead you to the information you want. They're equally important to content creators and search engines, helping to connect the right content with the right audience.

## More on Using Keywords Effectively

Let's look at keyword usage a bit more closely. We've mentioned the key places you should include your keywords, like the title tag, meta description, URL, headings, and within the content itself. But how do you do this effectively? Here are a few more tips:

- **First 100-150 words:** Try to include your keyword within the first 100-150 words of your content. This helps search engines quickly determine the topic of your content.

- **Last 100 words:** Similarly, using your keyword towards the end of your content can reinforce its main topic.

- **Keyword Frequency:** While it's important to include keywords throughout your content, avoid "keyword stuffing." That's when you overuse your keyword, making your content sound unnatural. This can actually hurt your SEO as search engines prefer content that's written for humans, not bots.

- **Synonyms and Variations:** Use synonyms and variations of your keyword to cover more ground. For example, if your keyword is "healthy dog food," variations could include "nutritious dog food," "dog food for health," or "healthy canine diet."

## Long-Tail Keywords and User Intent

We touched on long-tail keywords earlier, but they're so important that they deserve a bit more attention. These longer, more specific keyword phrases can be invaluable in reaching a more targeted audience and better matching user intent.

User intent is essentially what the searcher is really looking for when they type in a query. For example, if someone searches for "best dog food for a Labrador," they're likely looking for product recommendations or reviews. By using this long-tail keyword, you can create content that directly addresses this intent.

And that's a wrap on keywords, folks! Remember, using keywords effectively is like adding just the right amount of spice to your stew — it makes everything come together beautifully. Happy keywording, and see you in the next chapter!

## 4.5. Image Optimization

Ready to add a splash of color to your SEO adventure? That's right, it's time to talk about image optimization!

Just like the right GIF can make a tweet pop, the right image can make your web page more engaging and memorable.

But did you know that your images can also play a role in your SEO strategy? Let's dive in!

## Why Bother with Image Optimization?

Images can do more than just make your website look good. When properly optimized, they can also contribute to your site's visibility in search engine results. How, you ask? By improving page load times, enhancing user experience, and providing search engines with additional context about your page's content.

## Size Matters

First things first, let's talk about size. No, not the dimensions of the image, but its file size. Large image files can slow down your website, and a slow-loading website can send visitors bouncing back to the search results faster than a kangaroo on a trampoline.

To avoid this, it's a good idea to compress your images before uploading them to your website. There are plenty of free online tools that can help you with this, like TinyPNG or CompressJPEG.

## The Right Format

Next, consider the format of your image. The most common formats are JPEG, PNG, and GIF.

- JPEGs are great for photos or images with lots of colors.

- PNGs are perfect for images that require transparency, like logos.

- GIFs are your go-to for animations.

Choose the one that suits your needs while keeping file size in mind.

### Descriptive File Names

Here's a pro tip: before uploading an image, give its file a descriptive name. For example, instead of "IMG_1234.jpg", you might use "golden_retriever_puppy.jpg". This can help search engines understand what the image is about, and it can also help your image appear in image search results.

### Alt Text: The SEO Secret Weapon

Alt text (short for alternative text) is a brief description of an image, which is displayed if the image can't be loaded and is read by screen readers for visually impaired users. From an SEO perspective, alt text provides search engines with useful information about the image.

When writing alt text, try to be descriptive and, if it fits naturally, include your keyword.

**Caption This**

While not as important as alt text for SEO, image captions can be read by search engines and can help provide context. Plus, people tend to read captions when they scan through content, so a good caption can help engage your readers.

And there you have it – the colorful world of image optimization! Remember, every image on your website is an opportunity to improve your SEO and create a better user experience. So, go on and make your website picture-perfect! See you in the next chapter.

## 4.6. Mobile-Friendly Design

Because SEO isn't Just a Desktop Affair 😊

Hello again! Time to pocket that mouse, unplug that keyboard, and whip out your smartphones. Today, we're talking about mobile-friendly design. In a world where people Google from mountaintops and tweet from subways, making sure your website looks great and functions well on mobile devices is more important than ever. Let's dive into why this matters and how you can master it!

### Why Mobile-Friendly Design Matters

First things first: why should you care about mobile-friendly design? Well, for starters, more than half of all web traffic now comes from mobile devices. That's a lot of potential visitors! Moreover, search engines like Google have started to use mobile-first indexing.

This means they predominantly use the mobile version of your content for indexing and ranking. So, if your site isn't mobile-friendly, it's not just your users you're letting down - it's also your SEO.

### What is Mobile-Friendly Design?

Mobile-friendly design, also known as responsive design, means your website adjusts to look good and function well on any device, be it a desktop, a tablet, or a smartphone. This includes easy navigation, fast load times, readable text, and easy-to-tap buttons, among other things.

### The ABCs of Making Your Site Mobile-Friendly

Now, let's look at some key elements of a mobile-friendly design:

1. **Easy-to-Read Content:** On a smaller screen, readability is key. Make sure your text is large enough to read without squinting or zooming.

Break up your content into smaller chunks with headings and bullet points to make it more digestible.

2. **Touch-Friendly Navigation:** Those tiny links that are easy to click with a mouse can be frustratingly fiddly on a touchscreen. Make sure your buttons and links are large enough to tap easily with a finger.

3. **Optimized Images:** We talked about this in the last chapter, but it's worth repeating: large images can slow down your site. And on mobile, speed is even more crucial. So, optimize those images!

4. **Viewport Meta Tag:** This little piece of HTML code tells browsers to adjust the width and scaling of your page to fit the screen. If your site lacks this, it can lead to a frustrating experience for mobile users.

5. **Avoid Flash:** Many mobile browsers don't support Flash, so it's best to avoid it for essential elements of your site.

6. **Testing:** Last but not least, test your site on different devices and screen sizes to ensure it's truly mobile-friendly. Google's Mobile-Friendly Test tool can be a good starting point!

And there you have it – the ins and outs of mobile-friendly design! Remember, in today's on-the-go world, a mobile-friendly site isn't just nice to have – it's a must. So, go forth and make your website a place where every visitor feels at home, no matter what device they're using. Catch you in the next chapter!

## Let's test yourself!

**1. What does URL stand for?**

a) Underlying Resource Locator

b) Uniform Resource Locator

c) Universal Retrieval Link

d) Unique Resource Link

**2. What's the purpose of Meta Tags in SEO?**

a) To help decorate the webpage

b) To help search engines understand the content of a webpage

c) To help increase the loading speed of a webpage

d) To make the webpage look more colorful

**3. When optimizing content, where should your keyword ideally appear?**

a) Only in the conclusion

b) Just once in the middle of the content

c) In the first 100-150 words, and naturally throughout the content

d) As many times as possible, even if it sounds unnatural

**4. What is a long-tail keyword?**

a) A keyword that is longer than 10 characters

b) A keyword with a tail icon next to it

c) A specific keyword phrase that typically contains three or more words

d) A keyword related to animal tails

**5. Why should we optimize images on our website?**

a) To make the website more colorful

b) To make the images look good on Instagram

c) To improve page load times and provide search engines with additional context

d) Because everyone else is doing it

## 6. What is 'alt text' in image optimization?

a) An alternative text message service

b) A brief description of an image, displayed if the image can't load

c) The text you see when you hover over an image

d) A hidden message within the image

## 7. What percentage of web traffic comes from mobile devices?

a) Less than 10%

b) About 25%

c) More than 50%

d) 100%, because who uses desktops anymore?

## 8. What does a mobile-friendly design mean?

a) Making your website look cute on mobile phones

b) Ensuring your website adjusts to function well on any device

c) Designing your website only for mobile phones

d) Making your website look friendly and welcoming

## 9. What does the viewport meta tag do?

a) It allows you to see into the future

b) It tells browsers to adjust the width and scaling of your page to fit the screen

c) It tells your website how to behave in different climates

d) It helps to improve the resolution of your images

## 10. What tool can you use to test if your site is mobile-friendly?

a) Your best friend's smartphone

b) Google's Mobile-Friendly Test tool

c) The mobile phone of the person sitting next to you

d) Any phone from the mobile store

And how did it go? Don't forget to check your answers at the end of the book! 😊

# 5. Off-Page SEO

## 5.1. Link Building

Hello, SEO enthusiasts! Welcome to a brand-new chapter in our thrilling SEO guide. This time, we're stepping outside the cozy confines of your website and venturing into the great unknown: the world of off-page SEO. Our first stop?

The magical land of link building! Get ready to make friends, swap stories, and boost your website's authority like a pro. Let's go!

### What is Link Building?

Link building is the process of acquiring links from other websites that point back to your site. Think of these links as votes of confidence, telling search engines that your content is valuable and worth sharing. The more high-quality, relevant links you have, the more likely search engines are to view your site as an authority in your niche. This, in turn, can lead to higher rankings and more traffic.

### Why is Link Building Important?

Google and other search engines use links as a key factor in their ranking algorithms. In essence, they treat links like recommendations. If lots of reputable websites link to your content, it must be good, right? By building a strong link profile, you can improve your website's credibility and search engine rankings.

**Link Building Strategies: Making Friends the Right Way**

1. **Create Amazing Content:** It all starts here. If your content is valuable, informative, or entertaining, people will naturally want to link to it. Be the life of the SEO party with irresistible content that others can't help but share.

2. **Reach Out to Industry Influencers:** Don't be shy! Reach out to bloggers, journalists, and other influencers in your niche. Share your content with them and ask if they'd be willing to link to it if they find it valuable. Remember, flattery can go a long way – just be genuine and polite.

3. **Guest Posting:** Offer to write a guest post for another website in your niche. This can be a win-win situation: the host site gets free content, and you get a valuable backlink. Just make sure the site you're writing for is relevant and reputable.

4. **Build Relationships:** Networking is key in the world of link building. Join online communities,

forums, and social media groups related to your niche. Participate in discussions, share your expertise, and help others. As you build relationships, people will be more likely to link to your content.

5. **Broken Link Building:** Find broken links on other websites and suggest your own relevant content as a replacement. This can be a great way to gain a backlink while also helping the website owner fix their broken links. Win-win!

6. **Testimonials and Reviews:** Offer to write a testimonial or review for a product or service you've used, and ask if they'd be willing to link back to your site in return.

**A Word of Caution: Avoiding Bad Link Building Habits**

Not all link building strategies are created equal. Beware of spammy tactics or paying for low-quality backlinks, as these can harm your site's rankings in the long run. Stick to ethical, white-hat link building practices to ensure lasting success.

And there you have it – your introduction to the fabulous world of link building! As you embark on your off-page SEO journey, remember that it's all about building relationships and creating value for others. So, go forth and make friends – your website's authority and rankings will thank you!

## 5.2. Social Media and SEO

Today, we're going to take a thrilling journey into the bustling universe of social media and its powerful connection with SEO.

Yes, you heard it right! This chapter is all about how Facebook, Twitter, Instagram, and other social platforms can become a game-changer in your SEO strategy.

Ready to unlock the potential of social media for SEO? Buckle up, and let's roll!

### The Unseen Bond between Social Media and SEO

While social media signals don't directly impact your search engine rankings, social media and SEO are interwoven in ways that are hard to ignore. Imagine social media as your website's extroverted best friend at the party, introducing your content to potential fans across the globe.

Greater visibility means higher traffic, and increased traffic brings a higher chance of backlinks and shares, all of which sends positive signals to search engines about your website.

## Dance Steps to Synchronize Social Media with SEO

1. **Sharing is Caring:** The first step in your social media and SEO dance is to share your content on your social platforms. Every share is an invitation to your audience to visit your website, explore your content, and potentially link back to it from their own platforms.

2. **Engage Like There's No Tomorrow:** Social media isn't a one-way street; it's an interactive playground. Engage with your audience by responding to comments, participating in discussions, and fostering a sense of community. This not only enhances your brand's image but also drives more traffic to your website.

3. **Social Media for Link Building:** We all know how important backlinks are in the SEO world (remember our previous chapter?). Social media offers a powerful platform for networking with influencers, sharing your content, and earning those precious backlinks.

4. **Boost Your Content with Social Media Ads:** Got some marketing budget to spare? Try boosting your posts using social media advertising. This can put your content in front of a larger, more targeted audience, increasing your reach and potential for website traffic.

5. **Optimize Your Social Media Profiles:** Your social media profile is your digital storefront. Make sure to optimize it by including relevant keywords in your bio or about section, and, of course, always link back to your website.

6. **Use Hashtags Wisely:** Hashtags aren't just trendy; they're useful. They help categorize your content, making it easier for social media users to find. Just remember to use them sparingly and make sure they are relevant to your content.

7. **Leverage User-Generated Content:** Encourage your followers to share their own content related to your brand or products. User-generated content not only engages your audience but also gives you more content to share and can increase your brand's visibility.

**The Life of the Social Media Party: Fresh and Engaging Content**

In the world of social media, content is king, queen, and the whole court. Regularly sharing fresh, engaging content is the key to maintaining an active social media presence. But don't stress if you don't have time to create new content every day.

You can use ChatGPT, repurpose older content, share relevant content from others, or create new posts highlighting different aspects of your existing content.

And that's the extended tour of our Social Media and SEO exploration! Just remember, in the ever-evolving world of digital marketing, SEO and social media are two peas in a pod. They might not always directly interact, but when they work together, they can help your online presence soar.

Stay tuned for more exciting chapters on your journey to SEO mastery!

## 5.3. Content Marketing

Hello, future SEO gurus! It's time to turn the page to a new chapter in our exciting SEO journey. This time, we're stepping into the vibrant world of content marketing and discovering how it weaves into the broader tapestry of SEO.

Buckle up, because we're about to show how quality content can be the superpower that propels your website to the top of search engine results. Are you ready to become a content marketing maestro? Let's dive right in!

## Content Marketing and SEO: An Unbreakable Bond

Content marketing and SEO are like two sides of the same coin. While SEO focuses on making your website attractive to search engines, content marketing is all about appealing to human readers.

You see, search engines aim to deliver the most relevant and high-quality content to users, so by creating amazing content, you're helping search engines do their job!

## The Content Marketing Symphony: Key Elements

Creating quality content isn't just about writing well; it involves a symphony of elements that come together to form an engaging narrative. Let's discover what it takes to compose a masterpiece in content marketing:

1. **Understanding Your Audience:** Before you can create content that resonates, you need to know who you're talking to. Understand your audience's interests, needs, and challenges. This will help you create content that not only engages but also provides value.

2. **Keyword Research:** Just like in SEO, keywords play a starring role in content marketing. Use tools like Google Keyword Planner or Ahrefs to find relevant keywords that your audience is

searching for, and weave these into your content naturally.

3. **Creating Valuable Content:** This is the heart and soul of content marketing. From blog posts and articles to videos and infographics, your content should be designed to provide value, answer questions, solve problems, or entertain. Remember, quality over quantity is the golden rule!

4. **SEO Optimization:** Once you've crafted your amazing content, don't forget to optimize it for search engines. Include your keywords naturally, use meta tags, and structure your content for readability. Think back to our earlier chapters to refresh your memory on these crucial points!

5. **Promotion:** Writing great content is only half the battle; you also need to promote it. Share your content on social media, send it to your email list, and don't shy away from reaching out to influencers in your niche who might be interested in sharing your content too.

6. **Regular Updates:** The digital world moves at warp speed, and what was relevant yesterday might not be today. Regularly review and update your content to ensure it remains valuable, accurate, and SEO-friendly.

7. **Analyzing Performance:** Just like any marketing strategy, it's important to measure the performance of your content marketing efforts. Use tools like Google Analytics to see what's working and where there's room for improvement.

## The Power of Storytelling in Content Marketing

In content marketing, storytelling is your secret weapon. Stories have a unique power to engage readers, making your content more memorable and shareable. Whether you're sharing a case study, presenting data, or explaining a complex topic, try to weave a narrative that your audience can connect with.

And that concludes our deep-dive into content marketing! Remember, when it comes to winning at SEO, compelling, high-quality content is your most powerful ally.

So get out there, start creating, and let your content do the talking. Keep an eye out for our next chapter, where we'll continue unlocking the secrets of SEO. Until then, happy writing!

# Let's test yourself!

**1. If SEO and Content Marketing were at a zoo, which of the following best describes their relationship?**

a. They're like lions and gazelles – always at odds.

b. They're like squirrels and trees – one is always chasing the other.

c. They're like dolphins and water – you can't really have one without the other.

d. They're like penguins in the desert – they don't belong together.

**2. Why should you consider social media as your website's extroverted best friend at the party?**

a. Because social media always brings the best snacks.

b. Because social media introduces your content to potential fans across the globe, driving traffic to your website.

c. Because social media platforms make excellent DJs.

d. Because social media never forgets your birthday.

**3. What kind of links are considered the 'white chocolate' of the SEO world due to their importance and desirability?**

a. Chain links

b. Sausage links

c. Backlinks

d. Missing links

**4. If content is king in the world of Content Marketing, what could be considered the queen?**

a. Keyword stuffing

b. The latest meme

c. Value to the reader

d. Funny cat videos

**5. In the symphony of Content Marketing, what role does understanding your audience play?**

a. It's the conductor, guiding the whole performance.

b. It's the triangle player, only relevant occasionally.

c. It's the ticket booth, determining how many people show up.

d. It's the janitor, cleaning up after the performance.

Now check your answers at the end of the book!

# 6. Local SEO

## 6.1. Local SEO

Putting Your Business on the Map!

Hello, SEO lovers! We're back on the journey of discovery, and today we're talking about something a bit more... local. We're going to explore the bustling neighborhood of Local SEO! Grab your virtual maps and let's navigate the streets of this crucial aspect of search engine optimization.

### Local SEO: Your Friendly Neighborhood Spider-Man of SEO

So, what is Local SEO? Imagine SEO as a superhero. If SEO is Superman, flying around helping everyone worldwide, then Local SEO is more like your friendly neighborhood Spider-Man, focusing its superpowers on a specific locality – your business's neighborhood!

Local SEO is all about promoting your products and services to local customers at the exact time they're looking for them. It helps your business appear in local search results on search engines. Think about when you search for 'coffee shop near me'. The local coffee shops that pop up first? That's Local SEO working its magic!

## Why Local SEO Matters

Now, you might be wondering: "Why should I care about Local SEO?" The answer is simple – because your customers do! A significant portion of all Google searches are for local information.

Many users, who search for local businesses on mobile devices, call or visit these businesses shortly after their search.

Local SEO can make your business more visible in local search results, drive more traffic to your website, and ultimately lead to more customers – and who doesn't want more customers?

## The Key Components of Local SEO

Local SEO might seem like a big city to navigate, but don't worry – we've got your back! Here are some key landmarks to help you understand the local SEO landscape:

1. **Google My Business:** This is your home base in the world of Local SEO. It's a free tool from Google that lets you manage how your business appears in Google Search and Maps. It's like your business's own little superhero lair!

2. **Online Reviews:** These are like the citizens your superhero business is protecting. Positive reviews can help boost your business's visibility

and increase the likelihood that a potential customer will visit your location.

3. **Local Keywords:** These are your superpowers. Including location-based keywords in your website content can help improve your visibility in local search results.

So, there you have it – a friendly introduction to the world of Local SEO! It's a powerful tool to have in your SEO utility belt, especially for small businesses looking to make a big impact. Stay tuned for our next chapter, where we'll go deeper into the exciting world of SEO. Until then, happy optimizing!

## 6.2 Optimizing Google My Business

Hello again! So, we've established that Local SEO is like your friendly neighborhood superhero. Now, let's talk about your very own superhero headquarters – Google My Business (GMB). It's time to roll up our digital sleeves and get into the nitty-gritty of optimizing your GMB listing.

Ready? Let's dive right in!

**Google My Business: Your Local SEO Command Center**

Think of your Google My Business listing as your business's digital storefront. When people search for your business, it's often the first thing they see. It's like your business's digital ID card, displaying key information like your business name, address, hours, reviews, and more.

But a GMB listing is more than just an online directory. It's an interactive platform that can help boost your local SEO, attract more customers, and even allow you to engage with your audience directly. Cool, right?

**Optimizing Your GMB Listing: The Friendly Guide**

Optimizing your Google My Business listing is like decorating your superhero headquarters. You want to make sure it's functional, informative, and represents your business accurately. Here's how you can do it:

1. **Complete Your Profile:** Just like how a superhero needs their suit, your GMB listing needs complete information. Fill out every section – business name, address, phone number, website, hours, categories, and more. The more information you provide, the easier it is for customers to find and connect with you.

2. **Be Consistent:** Make sure the information on your GMB listing matches the information on your

website and other online directories. Consistency is key in the world of Local SEO.

3. **Add High-Quality Photos:** A picture is worth a thousand words, and that's certainly true for your GMB listing. High-quality photos of your business, products, or services can make your listing more engaging and attractive to potential customers.

4. **Collect and Respond to Reviews:** Encourage your customers to leave reviews on your GMB listing. Not only do reviews improve your local SEO, but they also build trust with potential customers. Remember to respond to reviews too – it's a great way to show you value customer feedback.

5. **Use Google Posts:** Google Posts are like mini-ads or social media posts that show up on your GMB listing. They're a great way to share updates, promotions, events, or news with people who find your business on Google.

6. **Analyze Insights:** Google provides valuable insights on how customers find your listing, what actions they take, and more. Use this data to understand your audience better and to make improvements to your listing.

And there you have it, friends – a friendly guide to optimizing your Google My Business listing. Remember, just like any superhero, your GMB listing is only as good as the effort you put into it. So, take the time to optimize it and watch as it helps boost your local SEO efforts!

## 6.3. Local Keywords

Hey there! Are you ready to discover another secret weapon in your Local SEO arsenal? Today, we're getting up close and personal with Local Keywords. Consider them your secret sauce, the magic words that can help your website pop up in local searches. Ready to sprinkle some of this magic onto your website? Let's dive in!

**Local Keywords: Your Secret Handshake with Search Engines**

First things first, what are local keywords? Well, they're pretty much like the keywords we've already talked about, but with a local twist. They include specific locations along with your target keywords. For example, if you're a pizza place in Brooklyn, your local keyword might be "best pizza in Brooklyn".

Using local keywords in your content is like a secret handshake with search engines. It tells them, "Hey, my business is here in this location!" This helps search engines match your website with local search queries, bringing more targeted traffic your way.

**Why Local Keywords are the Bees' Knees**

Now, you might wonder why you need to fuss about local keywords. Well, here's a fun fact: nearly half of all Google searches are for local information. And guess what? If your content is peppered with relevant local keywords, your business is more likely to show up in these searches. Sweet, right?

But the perks don't stop there! Local keywords also help you attract high-quality traffic. That's because people using local search terms are often ready to take action. So, if your content pops up when someone searches for "dog groomer in San Francisco", there's a good chance they're in need of your services right now!

**Finding and Using Local Keywords: A Friendly Guide**

Finding the right local keywords isn't a game of hide-and-seek. It's more of a treasure hunt! And like any good treasure hunt, you need the right tools and strategies. Here's a friendly guide to help you out:

1. **Think Like a Local:** Start by putting yourself in your customer's shoes. What terms would they use to search for your services in your area?

Don't forget to consider local slang and colloquialisms!

2. **Use Keyword Research Tools:** Tools like Google's Keyword Planner or Moz's Keyword Explorer can help you find popular local keywords related to your business.

3. **Check Out the Competition:** Look at what local keywords your competitors are using. You might discover some keyword goldmines!

4. **Implement Your Keywords:** Once you have your local keywords, sprinkle them throughout your website – in your titles, meta descriptions, headers, content, and even URLs. But remember, use them naturally. Keyword stuffing is a big no-no!

5. **Monitor and Adjust:** SEO is a marathon, not a sprint. Keep an eye on your analytics to see how your local keywords are performing and adjust as necessary.

With these magic words, you can help guide local customers right to your digital doorstep. Stay tuned for more exciting SEO adventures in our next chapter! Until then, happy optimizing!

# Let's test yourself!

**1. If Local SEO were a superhero, which of these would be its superpower?**

a) Flying around the world in seconds

b) Turning invisible

c) Helping your business appear in local search results

d) Time travel

**2. Your Google My Business listing is like:**

a) A dusty old phone book

b) A boring business meeting

c) Your business's digital ID card

d) A bowl of broccoli

**3. What's one way to optimize your Google My Business listing?**

a) Fill it with as many buzzwords as possible

b) Only include the bare minimum information

c) Fill out every section with accurate and consistent information

d) Ignore it and hope for the best

**4. What's a local keyword?**

a) A type of exotic bird

b) A key that opens all doors in your town

c) A keyword with your location added to it

d) A secret code to enter a local club

**5. How can you use local keywords to boost your local SEO?**

a) By stuffing as many as possible into your content

b) By ignoring them completely

c) By sprinkling them naturally throughout your website

d) By writing them in invisible ink

Hey, don't forget to check your answers at the end of the book!

# 7. Technical SEO

## 7.1. Page Load Speed

SEO virtuosos! Ever heard of the saying, "slow and steady wins the race"? Well, as much as we love a good tortoise-and-the-hare fable, that's not quite how things work in the land of SEO. When it comes to your website's load speed, being a Speedy Gonzales is the name of the game.

So, buckle up and let's zoom into the world of Page Load Speed!

### The Need for Speed in SEO-Land

Page Load Speed, in simple terms, is how quickly your webpage loads when someone clicks on your site. And guess what? Both your human visitors and the search engine bots have a need for speed.

Here's why: people are busy. They want to find what they're looking for quickly and easily. If your page takes too long to load, they're likely to hit the back button faster than you can say 'SEO'. In fact, studies show that a delay of just one second in page response can result in a 7% reduction in conversions. Yikes!

And it's not just your visitors who appreciate a speedy site. Search engines do, too. Google, for example, considers page load speed as one of its ranking factors. A faster site can lead to better visibility in search results. That's a win-win!

## Tools to Check and Improve Page Speed

Now, you might be thinking, "How do I know if my website is a speed demon or a slow poke?" That's where tools come in handy. There are several great free tools out there that not only measure your site's speed but also give you insights on how to improve it.

Google's PageSpeed Insights is one such tool. It scores your page on a scale of 0 to 100 and offers suggestions for improvement. Another tool is GTMetrix, which provides a comprehensive look at your page's speed performance. Pingdom is another popular choice that provides easy-to-understand reports.

## Turbocharging Your Page Load Speed

So, how do you go about speeding up your website? Here are a few friendly tips:

1. **Optimize Your Images:** Big, bulky images can slow down your site. Use tools to compress your images without losing quality, and consider using a format like JPEG 2000, JPEG XR, or WebP that provides superior compression.

2. **Minify CSS, JavaScript, and HTML:** By optimizing your code (including removing spaces, commas, and other unnecessary characters), you can increase your page speed.

3. **Reduce Redirects:** Each time a page redirects to another page, your visitor faces additional time waiting for the HTTP request-response cycle to complete.

4. **Leverage Browser Caching:** Browsers cache a lot of information (like stylesheets, images, JavaScript files, etc.) so that when a visitor comes back to your site, the browser doesn't have to reload the entire page.

5. **Use a Content Distribution Network (CDN):** CDNs are networks of servers that are used to distribute the load of delivering content. Essentially, copies of your site are stored at multiple, geographically diverse data centers so users have faster and more reliable access to your site.

Remember, the need for speed isn't just about keeping the search engine bots happy. It's about creating a better, smoother experience for your users. And a happy user is much more likely to become a loyal customer. So, put on your speed goggles, fire up your engines, and let's make your website the Speedy Gonzales of the SEO-land!

## 7.2. Clean Code

Ready to roll up your sleeves and get your hands a little dirty? Don't worry, we're not talking about gardening. Today, we're diving deep into the heart of your website – the code. It's time to learn the art of tidying up... our code, that is! Let's dive in.

### Clean Code, Happy Website

In the world of programming, 'clean code' is code that is easy to understand, easy to read, and easy to maintain. It's code that's written in a way that's consistent, logical, and efficient. Clean code is like a well-organized closet – everything has its place, and there's no unnecessary clutter.

Why does this matter for SEO? Well, search engine bots are like speedy little librarians. They 'read' your website's code to understand what your site is about and where to rank it in search results.

If your code is clean and well-organized, these bots can zip through it quickly and easily. But if your code is messy and cluttered, it can slow down these bots and even confuse them. And a confused bot is not a happy bot.

**Tidying Up Your Code**

So, how do you tidy up your code? Here are a few friendly tips:

1. **Minify Your Code:** Minifying your code means removing unnecessary characters (like spaces and line breaks) and simplifying it as much as possible without changing its functionality. It's like decluttering your closet – you're getting rid of anything you don't need.

2. **Use Semantic HTML:** This means using HTML tags in a way that represents the content contained in them. For example, using **<header>**, **<footer>**, and **<article>** tags for your header, footer, and article content, respectively. This helps search engine bots understand your content better.

3. **Remove Duplicate Code:** If you have the same chunk of code in multiple places, it's time to consolidate. Having duplicate code is like having two identical black shirts in your closet – one is enough!

4. **Keep Your CSS External:** This means storing your CSS code in an external file and linking to it from your HTML. This makes your HTML file cleaner and easier to read.

**Tools for Cleaning Up**

Thankfully, you don't have to tidy up your code by hand. There are several tools out there that can help. For minifying your code, try tools like UglifyJS (for JavaScript) or CSSNano (for CSS). For finding and removing duplicate code, try tools like JSCPD or CSSLint.

These tools function like a personal organizing expert, aiding you in decluttering and structuring your code for a more efficient, happier website.

So, there you have it – the art of clean code for SEO. Remember, a tidy website is a happy website, and a happy website ranks better in search results. So, let's roll up our sleeves, grab our tools, and start tidying up!

Keep an eye out for more technical SEO insights in our next chapter. Until then, happy coding!

# 7.3. Using the robots.txt File

Have you ever thought about what would happen if you had a bouncer for your website? Someone who could tell the search engine bots where they can and can't go? Well, that's exactly what the robots.txt file does! Consider it as the friendly bouncer of your website. Intrigued? Let's get to know this bouncer a little better!

## Meet Your Website's Bouncer: robots.txt

In the world of SEO, the robots.txt file is a simple text file that tells search engine bots which pages or sections of your site they should visit and which ones they should steer clear of. This might seem a bit counterintuitive. After all, don't we want search engines to see all our amazing content?

Well, yes and no. While we want search engines to index most of our pages, there might be some sections of our site we'd rather keep private. For example, you might have an admin page or a personal directory that doesn't need to be indexed. That's where our friendly bouncer, robots.txt, steps in.

## Setting Up Your robots.txt

Setting up your robots.txt file is as easy as pie! It's just a simple text file that lives in the root directory of your site. You can do this manually or use a plugin if you have a website built in WordPress. In this chapter, we will present you with two methods, so if the first one intimidates you, don't worry - the plugin will come to your rescue!

Here's what a basic robots.txt file might look like:

javascriptCopy code

User-agent: * Disallow: /private/

In this example, "User-agent: *" means this section applies to all robots, and "Disallow: /private/" tells the robots not to crawl anything in the private directory of the site.

**A Few Friendly Tips**

While robots.txt is a powerful tool, it's also a sensitive one. A small error could accidentally block search engines from your entire site, which is a bit like having a bouncer who won't let anyone into the club! So, here are a few friendly tips:

1. **Be Precise:** Make sure you're only blocking the parts of your site you mean to block.

2. **Check Regularly:** Google Search Console has a "robots.txt Tester" tool which can help you check for errors.

3. **No Secrets:** Remember, robots.txt is publicly available. So, don't use it to hide sensitive information.

By guiding search engines through your site more effectively, it helps you make the most of your SEO efforts.

# I.   Creating Your Robots.txt File – Method 1 (Manual)

First things first, you'll need to create your robots.txt file. Remember, this is just a simple text file, so you can create it using any text editor like Notepad on Windows or TextEdit on Mac. Here's a step-by-step guide:

1. Open your text editor of choice and create a new file.

2. Start with the line "User-agent: *". This line tells the robots.txt file that the instructions that follow apply to all bots.

3. On the next line, you can start adding your instructions. If you want to disallow bots from a certain directory, you would write "Disallow: /directory-name/".

4. Save this file as "robots.txt".

Voila! You have created your robots.txt file.


**Adding Your Robots.txt File to Your Website**

Now that you've got your shiny new robots.txt file, it's time to add it to your website. For this, you'll need access to your website's root directory. This is usually done through a FTP client or your web host's file manager. Here's how you can do it:

1. Connect to your website's root directory using your FTP client or your web host's file manager.

2. Look for your public_html folder. This is usually the root directory for your website.

3. Upload your robots.txt file to this directory.

And just like that, your robots.txt file is live!

Once you've added your robots.txt file to your website, you can check to make sure it's working by going to www.yourwebsite.com/robots.txt. You should see the contents of your robots.txt file there.

Remember, the robots.txt file is a powerful tool, but it needs to be used with care. A misplaced "Disallow: /" could block search engines from your entire site! So always double-check your work and test your robots.txt file with Google's robots.txt Tester tool.

## II.      WordPress Plugins to the Rescue – Method 2 (Plugin)

If the thought of manually creating and uploading a robots.txt file feels a bit intimidating, don't worry, our favorite website platform - WordPress - comes to our rescue! There are several WordPress plugins that can help you manage your robots.txt file right from your WordPress dashboard. Isn't that cool?

1. **Yoast SEO:** This well-loved SEO plugin doesn't just help with your meta tags and sitemaps, it can also assist with your robots.txt file. Once you've installed and activated Yoast SEO, you can navigate to SEO > Tools > File editor to create or modify your robots.txt file.

2. **All in One SEO Pack:** Another crowd favorite, All in One SEO Pack also offers tools to manage your robots.txt file. After installation, you can find this feature under Feature Manager > Robots.txt.

3. **Virtual Robots.txt:** This plugin is specifically designed for managing your robots.txt file. It automatically creates a virtual robots.txt file, and you can modify it directly from the Settings > Reading screen in your WordPress dashboard.

Remember, while these plugins make managing your robots.txt file easier, it's still crucial to ensure you're using the correct syntax and not blocking any important pages or directories. Always double-check your work and test your robots.txt file with Google's robots.txt Tester tool.

There you go, my WordPress-loving friends! With these plugins, managing your robots.txt file is as easy as pie. Until next time, happy plugin installing

## 7.4. XML Sitemap

Ahoy! Imagine you're on a quest for hidden treasure. You wouldn't just wander around aimlessly, would you? No, you'd use a map to find the quickest path to the loot! Similarly, search engines need a map to find all the valuable content on your website. This map is called an XML Sitemap.

Let's jump aboard the good ship 'SEO' and set sail for the island of XML Sitemaps!

**Decoding the XML Sitemap**

In the simplest terms, an XML Sitemap is a file that lists all important pages of your website, helping Google and other search engines find your content and understand the structure of your site. It's like giving them a cheat sheet to all the good stuff on your website!

Think of it like the table of contents for your website. It provides search engines with a clear guide to all the significant parts, ensuring they don't miss anything important. As before, here we also have two methods for creating such a map - manual and automatic using a plugin.

## I.  Creating the XML Sitemap – Method 1 (Manual)

Let's dive into the world of manual XML sitemap creation! Now, it might seem a bit technical at first, but don't worry. We'll walk through it step by step. Ready? Let's get to it!

**Step 1: Create a New Text Document** You'll start off by opening a text editor. This could be Notepad if you're on Windows, or TextEdit if you're on a Mac. Create a new document.

**Step 2: Start with the Basic Code** Every XML sitemap begins with the same basic code. You'll want to copy and paste this code into your text document:

xmlCopy code

```
<?xml version="1.0" encoding="UTF-8"?> <urlset xmlns="http://www.sitemaps.org/schemas/sitemap/0.9"> </urlset>
```

This code defines your document as an XML file and starts your URL list.

**Step 3: Add Your URLs** Now, it's time to add your URLs. For each URL, you'll want to include a <url> tag with the

<loc> tag containing the actual URL. It'll look something like this:

xmlCopy code

<url>        <loc>http://www.example.com/example-page/</loc> </url>

Repeat this process for each URL you want to include in your sitemap. Just remember, the URLs should be between the <urlset> and </urlset> tags.

**Step 4: Save Your File** Once you've added all your URLs, save your file with the .xml extension. Your filename should be sitemap.xml.

### Step 5: Upload Your Sitemap

Now that you've created your sitemap, you need to upload it to your website's root directory. This directory is essentially the heart of your website where all the main files reside. Usually, it's named as 'public_html' or 'www'.

1.  Access your website's files. You can usually do this via an FTP client like FileZilla or through your web host's file manager. If you're unsure, your hosting provider can guide you.

2.  Locate the root directory. Look for a folder named 'public_html' or 'www'.

3. Upload your 'sitemap.xml' file. Simply drag and drop the file into the root directory if you're using an FTP client, or use the upload function in your web host's file manager.

Now, your sitemap is living right at the heart of your website, ready to guide search engines to all your great content!

Remember, the URL to access the sitemap will be something like: http://www.yourwebsite.com/sitemap.xml.

**Step 6: Submit Your Sitemap to Google** The final step is to submit your sitemap to Google via Google Search Console. Just click on 'Sitemaps' in the left-hand menu, enter the URL of your sitemap, and hit 'Submit'.

And there you go! You've successfully created and submitted your very own XML sitemap! Remember, creating your sitemap manually gives you full control over what gets included, but it does require updating manually as well. So, if your site changes often, you may want to consider an automatic sitemap generator tool.

Congratulations on your new XML sitemap! Keep exploring, brave SEO adventurer!

## II.    Creating Your XML Sitemap – Method 2 (Plugin)

Creating an XML Sitemap might sound like a daunting task, but it's actually a smooth sail with the right tools. There are numerous online tools and plugins that can generate an XML Sitemap for you. Here are a few of our favorites:

1. **Yoast SEO:** Our trusty WordPress plugin friend is back! If you're using WordPress, Yoast SEO can automatically generate an XML Sitemap for you. Simply navigate to SEO > General > Features and ensure that the 'XML sitemaps' toggle is set to 'On'.

2. **Google XML Sitemaps:** This is another fantastic WordPress plugin that can create a sitemap for you. Once installed, it automatically generates an XML Sitemap and keeps it updated as you add new content.

3. **Screaming Frog:** This SEO tool isn't just for identifying issues with your site – it can also generate an XML Sitemap! It's perfect for those who prefer a desktop application over a web-based one.

**Submitting Your XML Sitemap to Google**

Once you've created your XML Sitemap, it's time to submit it to Google via the Google Search Console. This process is like handing over your treasure map to the search engines. Here's how to do it:

1. Log into your Google Search Console account.

2. Select your website property.

3. Click on 'Sitemaps' on the left-hand menu.

4. Enter the URL of your sitemap and click 'Submit'.

Voila! You've successfully submitted your XML Sitemap to Google!

And there you have it – the mysterious XML Sitemap, decoded! Remember, your XML Sitemap is a critical tool in your SEO toolbox, guiding search engines to your website's most valuable content. Keep it updated, submit it to Google, and you'll be well on your way to SEO success!

## 7.5. HTTPS and SSL Certificates

Hello there, budding SEO enthusiast! Today we're going to talk about something super important – HTTPS and SSL Certificates. Think of them as the trusty locks and alarm systems for your website.

They help keep information secure and tell your visitors (and search engines) that your site is safe and trustworthy.

### What's the deal with HTTPS and SSL?

HTTPS stands for 'Hyper Text Transfer Protocol Secure', which is just a fancy way of saying it's a more secure version of HTTP, the protocol used to send data between your website and a visitor's browser.

The magic behind HTTPS is something called SSL, or 'Secure Sockets Layer'. SSL Certificates encrypt data sent between browsers and servers, making it more difficult for bad guys to steal sensitive information.

When a site uses an SSL Certificate and HTTPS, you'll usually see a little padlock symbol next to the URL in your browser, which is a visible sign that the site is secure.

**Why do HTTPS and SSL matter for SEO?**

Google has been using HTTPS as a ranking signal since 2014. That means having a secure site can actually help your SEO! Plus, visitors are more likely to trust and interact with sites that are secure.

**How to Switch to HTTPS and Install an SSL Certificate**

1. **Purchase an SSL Certificate:** These are issued by Certificate Authorities (CAs). You can often buy them directly through your hosting company, or from third-party sellers like Comodo, DigiCert, or Symantec.

2. **Install the SSL Certificate:** The installation process varies based on your web host. Some hosts offer easy tools or support to install your certificate. If you're unsure, check with your hosting provider's help center or contact their support team.

3. **Switch Your Site to HTTPS:** Once the certificate is installed, you'll need to update your site settings to use HTTPS. In WordPress, for example, you'd go to Settings > General and update your WordPress and Site Address to use HTTPS. You can also use plugin like 'Really Simple SSL' if you're using WordPress.

4. **Set up 301 Redirects:** You want to make sure any traffic to your old HTTP site is automatically redirected to your new HTTPS site. You can do this in your .htaccess file, or with a plugin like 'Really Simple SSL' if you're using WordPress.

5. **Update Google Analytics and Google Search Console:** If you use these tools, remember to update your settings there to use the HTTPS version of your site.

And there you have it! You've just leveled up your website's security and SEO. Remember, having a secure site is not just good for rankings, it's great for building trust with your visitors too. Keep up the good work!

## Let's test yourself!

**1. What does HTTPS stand for?**

a) Hyper Text Transfer Protocol Super

b) Hyper Text Transfer Protocol Secure

c) Hey There, That's Pretty Secure

d) Honestly, That's Too Specific

**2. What do we use robots.txt for?**

a) To organize robot dance parties

b) To track robot activity on our site

c) To feed the Google bots so they don't get hungry

d) To tell search engine bots what parts of our site to crawl

**3. Why should we care about page load speed?**

a) Because slow pages are just plain annoying

b) Because faster pages generally rank higher in search engine results

c) Because we're in a hurry

d) Both a) and b)

**4. What is the purpose of an XML Sitemap?**

a) It's a treasure map leading to hidden internet gold

b) It helps search engines understand the structure of our website

c) It's a map for website visitors

d) It's an X-Men Locator

## 5. What is 'clean code'?

a) Code that has been scrubbed with soap

b) Code that is easy for humans and machines to understand

c) Code without any bugs

d) Code that has been approved by the Clean Code Council

## 6. Where should you upload your XML sitemap?

a) To your favorite social media site

b) To your website's root directory

c) To the Sitemap Museum

d) Anywhere, as long as you have a good internet connection

## 7. Why is it important to switch to HTTPS?

a) It's a trend, everybody's doing it

b) It's necessary for using certain web technologies

c) It helps protect your site's data and boosts your SEO

d) HTTP is so 1990s

**8. What is one way to improve your site's load speed?**

a) Yelling at your computer

b) Optimizing image sizes

c) Adding more plugins to your website

d) Inviting more visitors to your website


**9. What is the purpose of an SSL Certificate?**

a) It establishes a secure connection between a user's web browser and your website

b) It's a certificate you get for being a Super Smart Learner

c) It's for bragging rights

d) It's a decoration for your website's homepage

Now it's time to check your answers at the end of the book!

# 8. SEO Analysis and Monitoring

## 8.1. Tools for Tracking SEO Results

When you're working hard on your SEO, it's just like planting a garden. You wouldn't just plant seeds and walk away, right? You'd want to check on your little sprouts, make sure they're growing, and see if any pesky weeds (aka, SEO problems) need pulling. That's where SEO tracking tools come into play.

1. **Google Analytics:** This is like your basic garden toolset – it's essential for any website owner. Google Analytics lets you see how many people are visiting your site, where they're coming from, what pages they're visiting, and even what they had for breakfast. Okay, maybe not that last one, but it's still super informative!

2. **Google Search Console:** This is like your garden health report. It helps you understand how Google's search bots see your site, and it can point out any problems or issues that might be affecting your SEO. It's also the tool you'll use to submit your sitemap and see which keywords are leading people to your site.

3. **SEMRush or Ahrefs:** These tools are like your garden encyclopedia. They provide a wealth of information about your site's SEO performance,

including keyword rankings, backlink analysis, competitor analysis, and more. They are premium tools, but they offer free versions with limited functionality which can be enough for beginners.

4. **Moz Pro:** Another great all-in-one SEO toolkit is Moz Pro. It's like having your own personal garden advisor. With Moz, you can track your keyword rankings, analyze your on-page SEO, check for technical issues, and more.

5. **Screaming Frog SEO Spider:** This tool is the trusty garden hoe that helps you dig deep into your site's SEO. It's a website crawler that checks for common SEO issues, like broken links, duplicate content, and more.

Remember, SEO isn't a one-and-done deal. It's an ongoing process, like tending a garden. So, equip yourself with the right tools, and you'll be well on your way to a thriving website. Happy gardening, my friends!

## 8.2. Interpreting Data from Google Analytics

Think of Google Analytics as your website's diary. It keeps a record of all the people who visit, where they come from, what they do while they're hanging out, and even when they decide to leave. Our goal is to understand this diary and use it to make our website an even better place to visit.

1. **Audience Overview:** This is like the guest book of your website. It shows you how many people have visited (sessions), how many were first-time visitors (new users), and how many have visited before (returning users). It's a great way to see how popular your website is and if people enjoy their time enough to come back.

2. **Acquisition Overview:** Ever wondered how people found your website? The Acquisition Overview is your answer! It shows you how your traffic gets to you. It could be through search engines (organic search), through a link on another website (referral), directly by typing in your URL (direct), or from social media sites (social). This way, you know what's working and where to focus your efforts.

3. **Behavior Overview:** This section is like the guest survey of your website. It shows what pages your visitors are checking out

(pageviews), which page they see first (landing pages), and which page they see last before they leave (exit pages). This can help you see what content is most popular and where you might be losing people.

4. **Conversions:** If your website has a specific goal, like selling a product or getting sign-ups for a newsletter, this is the section for you. It tracks how many visitors complete the goal (conversions) and where they came from. This is super important for understanding if your website is doing its job.

5. **Real-Time Reports:** Want to know what's happening on your site right now? Like, this very second? Then check out the Real-Time reports. You can see how many people are on your site, what pages they're viewing, where they're from, and more. It's like having a live CCTV feed of your website's activity.

6. **Bounce Rate:** Imagine inviting people to a party, and they leave without even saying hello. That's what a high bounce rate feels like. It's the percentage of single-page sessions, meaning the visitor left your site from the entrance page without interacting with it. A high bounce rate could indicate that your site isn't engaging enough or doesn't match what the visitor expected.

7. **Session Duration:** This is the amount of time visitors spend on your site. It's like the length of time guests stay at your party. Longer session durations typically mean that visitors are finding your content engaging and valuable.

8. **Demographics and Interests:** Who are the people visiting your website? Are they young, old, male, female? Are they into sports, fashion, technology? Google Analytics can tell you. This information can be super valuable when creating content and targeting your audience.

9. **Site Speed:** This tells you how quickly your website loads for your visitors. If it's slow, people might be leaving before your content even has a chance to load. Google Analytics gives you data on your site's speed and even offers suggestions on how to make it faster.

10. **Mobile Overview:** With more and more people browsing the web on their phones, it's crucial to know how many of your visitors are coming from mobile devices. This report can help you understand how well your site is performing for mobile users.

Remember, data is power, but only if you understand what it's telling you. So take your time, dig in, and let the Google Analytics data be your guide. You've got this, my friends!

## 8.3. Regular SEO Reviews and Updates

SEO isn't a set-it-and-forget-it kind of thing. It's more like taking care of a lovely garden. You've got to keep watering, pruning, and checking on those plants regularly. So, let's grab our gardening gloves and dig into how to keep our SEO garden thriving.

**1. Regular SEO Audits:** An SEO audit is like a health checkup for your website. It's a way to see how well your site is performing in terms of SEO and to identify any areas that might need some TLC. Tools like SEMrush, Ahrefs, and Google Search Console can help you run these audits. Ideally, you should be doing an SEO audit every six months.

**2. Stay Updated:** Just like fashion trends, SEO trends can change quickly. What worked last year might not work this year. So, make sure you stay updated with the latest SEO news and updates. Follow SEO blogs, attend webinars, participate in SEO forums – immerse yourself in the SEO world.

**3. Regularly Update Content:** If your content is outdated, it's less likely to rank high in search engine results. Regularly review and update your content to keep it fresh, relevant, and valuable for your visitors. This could mean updating stats, adding new information, or even rewriting sections to improve readability.

**4. Monitor Your Competitors:** Keep an eye on what your competitors are doing. If they suddenly start ranking higher than you for certain keywords, take a look at what they're doing differently. Maybe they've updated their content, improved their site speed, or started using new keywords. Learn from them and adapt.

**5. Keep Checking Your Site Speed:** Slow and steady does not win the race when it comes to website loading times. Regularly check your site speed to ensure your visitors aren't left waiting. Use tools like Google's PageSpeed Insights for this.

**6. Regular Backlink Checks:** Backlinks are a key part of SEO. Regularly check who's linking to you, ensure the links are still active, and aim to continuously generate high-quality backlinks.

**7. Mobile Optimization Checks:** With an increasing number of users browsing the web on their mobile devices, it's essential to ensure your website is mobile-friendly. Regularly test your site on various devices and screen sizes and make necessary adjustments to improve the mobile user experience.

**8. Keyword Position Tracking:** Keeping an eye on where your keywords rank in search engine results is important. If you notice a drop in rankings for a particular keyword, it may be time to revisit your content or keyword strategy. Tools like Ahrefs and SEMrush can help you track keyword positions over time.

**9. Regularly Check and Update Meta Tags:** Meta tags like meta titles and descriptions play a crucial role in SEO. Make it a habit to regularly review and update these as needed to ensure they're effectively telling search engines (and users) what your content is about.

**10. Monitor User Behavior with Analytics:** Use Google Analytics or similar tools to track how users are interacting with your site. Which pages have the highest bounce rate? Where do users spend the most time? This information can guide your SEO strategy and highlight areas for improvement.

Remember, SEO is a journey, not a destination. There's always something new to learn, something to improve, or a new strategy to try. So, keep growing, keep learning, and keep making your website the best it can be. Happy SEOing!

# Let's test yourself!

**1. What's the best way to view your website the way a search engine sees it?**

a. Through a magic crystal ball

b. With a pair of binoculars

c. Using Google URL Inspection Tool

d. With X-ray glasses

**2. Which tool can you use to check your website's loading speed?**

a. A stopwatch

b. Your cousin who claims he counts super fast

c. Google's PageSpeed Insights

d. An egg timer

**3. How often should you perform an SEO audit on your website?**

a. Once in a blue moon

b. Whenever you feel like it

c. Every six months

d. Only when your website crashes

**4. When checking data in Google Analytics, a high bounce rate is...**

a. A sign that your website is a trampoline

b. The result of too many bouncy balls on your site

c. Indicative of users leaving your site after viewing only one page

d. A statistic that only applies to basketball-related websites

**5. What is the importance of keeping your content up to date?**

a. So that it doesn't get lonely

b. To keep it fresh, relevant, and valuable for your visitors

c. Because old content will start to smell

d. To maintain a good relationship with the content fairy

Remember to check your answers at the end of the book!

# 9. The Future of SEO

## 9.1. Latest Trends in SEO

Hey there, SEO enthusiast! Buckle up because we're about to take a thrilling ride into the future of SEO. As you've probably noticed, the digital landscape is constantly changing, and the world of SEO is no exception. So, let's see what's trending in the SEO cosmos right now!

**1. Core Web Vitals:** Google's Page Experience Update has brought Core Web Vitals into the spotlight. These vitals, which include Largest Contentful Paint (LCP), First Input Delay (FID), and Cumulative Layout Shift (CLS), are all about providing a great user experience. So it's time to ensure your website is up to speed, interactive, and visually stable!

**2. Voice Search:** With the rise of virtual assistants like Siri, Alexa, and Google Assistant, voice search is becoming increasingly popular. This trend calls for a shift towards long-tail keywords and a conversational tone in your content. Hey Siri, how cool is that?

**3. Mobile-First Indexing:** Google now uses the mobile version of your site for indexing and ranking. So, if your site isn't mobile-friendly, it's high time to make it so!

**4. EEAT (Experience, Expertise, Authoritativeness, and Trustworthiness):** Google is emphasizing the importance of quality content that demonstrates EEAT. This is especially crucial for YMYL (Your Money or Your Life) topics. So, let's serve up some high-quality, trustworthy content!

**5. Video SEO:** Videos are engaging and can keep visitors on your site longer, which can be a big plus for your SEO. Platforms like YouTube also offer another way to get your content noticed. So, lights, camera, action on your video content!

**6. Featured Snippets:** These are the short snippets of text that appear at the top of Google's search results in order to quickly answer a searcher's query. They're also known as "Position 0" in the search results. Learning how to optimize for these can give you a significant visibility boost on search engine results pages (SERPs).

**7. Semantic Search:** Search engines are getting better at understanding the context of content. They can now interpret the intent of a user's search query for more accurate results, beyond simply matching keywords. It's becoming more important to write content in a natural, conversational language and to focus on topics rather than specific keywords.

**8. Local SEO and Google My Business:** If you're running a local business, optimizing for local search results is crucial. Make sure your Google My Business page is set up and kept up-to-date with your current address, opening hours, and customer reviews.

**9. User Experience (UX) and SEO:** Google is putting more emphasis on the overall user experience. This means factors such as website speed, mobile-friendliness, easy navigation, and high-quality content are more important than ever. A good user experience can lead to better engagement rates, which can positively impact your SEO.

**10. AI and Machine Learning:** Google's AI algorithm, RankBrain, is getting better at understanding context and user intent. Other tools are using AI for content creation, keyword research, and more. Now that ChatGPT has been created, each of us can utilize artificial intelligence for SEO activities. In the next chapter, you'll learn more about it! Keep reading and don't get left behind!

Remember, SEO isn't a one-time task – it's an ongoing process. These trends will continue to evolve and keeping up with them will help you stay ahead of the curve. Happy optimizing!

## 9.2 ChatGPT & other AI tools in SEO

Hello there, future SEO superstars! In this chapter, we're going to talk about a real game-changers – ChatGPT & other AI tools. They're going to be your new best friends in the SEO world. No worries, we'll explain everything in an easy-to-understand way, even if you're just starting out!

### What is ChatGPT?

Let's start with the basics. ChatGPT is an artificial intelligence program that can generate human-like text based on the prompts given to it. Think of it like a very smart chatbot that can talk about pretty much anything (chat.openai.com). Cool, huh?

## How Can ChatGPT Help with SEO?

Well, it's magic... Just kidding, but it is magical in its own way. ChatGPT can be used to write SEO-optimized content, suggest keyword strategies, provide insights on trending topics – all of which can boost your SEO efforts. And guess what? It does this all in seconds, saving you a ton of time.

### 1. Content Creation

ChatGPT can draft SEO-friendly content like blog posts, product descriptions, or landing pages. Give it a topic and some keywords, and you have content ready in no time. Remember, quality content is key in SEO, and that's what ChatGPT is good at!

### 2. Keyword Suggestions

Wondering what keywords to use for your content? ChatGPT can help with that too. Tell it about your business or topic, and it'll generate a list of relevant keywords. And voila! You're on your way to SEO greatness.

### 3. Long-Tail Keyword Generation

Long-tail keywords are more specific and less competitive than shorter, more general keywords. ChatGPT can help you generate long-tail keywords that are relevant to your content, making it easier for you to rank high in these specific niche areas.

### 4. Trending Topics

Keeping up with trends is important in SEO. But don't sweat it, ChatGPT has your back. It can generate a list of trending topics in your niche. Now you can easily craft content that resonates with your audience.

### 5. Meta-Data Optimization

Metadata, like page titles and meta descriptions, are key SEO elements. ChatGPT can assist in creating compelling and effective metadata that attracts users and improves your search engine rankings. Just give it a clear description of your webpage and let it craft SEO-friendly metadata for you.

### 6. Competitive Analysis

Analyzing what your competitors are doing right is an important part of SEO. ChatGPT can help you generate a list of elements to check on your competitors' sites such as keyword usage, content length and quality, backlinks, and more.

### 7. User Experience Optimization

Great user experience is increasingly becoming a significant factor in SEO. ChatGPT can generate guidelines on how to enhance the user experience of your site, from mobile optimization and load speed to site navigation and layout.

### 8. Backlink Outreach

Backlinks are a big deal in SEO. ChatGPT can help you draft personalized outreach emails or messages for link building – building relationship with other websites. Just give it the details you want to include, and you'll have a friendly, professional message ready to go.

## Time and Efficiency

Forget about hours spent brainstorming and drafting. With ChatGPT, you get fast, efficient, and consistent help. So, you can focus more on the other aspects of your business.

Using ChatGPT can significantly speed up our work, but conversing with it and using the correct commands is not easy. Initially, it can lead to frustration, below you will find the most important rules for writing commands.

Also remember that what ChatGPT gives you is not always correct – always thoroughly check everything before you publish anything! ChatGPT is incredibly helpful, it's like our assistant, but it also makes mistakes. Always carefully read what you receive from it!

# How to write prompts to ChatGPT – in a nutshell:

1.  **Be Specific:** Try to be as specific as possible in your prompts. If you need information about a specific topic, make sure to include that topic in your question.

2.  **Set the Tone:** When asking for a text, define the style you want it in - whether it's formal, casual, humorous, serious, etc.

3.  **Context Matters:** Provide necessary context in your prompts. If the conversation involves previous discussion points, make sure they are clear for the model to understand.

4.  **Directly Ask:** If you need a specific type of response, like a bullet list or a summary, directly ask for it in the prompt.

5.  **Role-Play:** You can assign roles to the AI, like 'You are a tour guide,' or 'You are a copywriter with 10 years' experience' and it will respond accordingly.

6.  **Try Different Approaches:** If you're not getting the response you want, try asking the question in a different way.

7. **Experiment and Learn:** Not every prompt will work perfectly the first time. It's important to experiment and learn from your interactions with the model.

## Other AI tools in SEO

ChatGPT is not the only tool available for generating SEO content. There are many specialized AI tools designed specifically for this purpose that you can find online. It's important to note that while some of these tools offer advanced features and capabilities, they often come with a price tag.

Check various tools - both free and paid - as it may turn out that the free ones are sufficient, or it may be worth paying for the paid ones because the quality of the provided features is much higher.

In the dynamic world of SEO, AI doesn't stop at text generation. Several other tools, driven by AI, can streamline and supercharge your SEO efforts. For instance, AI-powered image and video generators can create visually engaging content that improves user experience and boosts dwell time.

These tools use machine learning algorithms to produce high-quality, unique visuals based on user-defined parameters, saving both time and creative energy.

Similarly, AI-driven SEO analysis tools can provide deep insights into your website's performance, offering precise recommendations for optimization. From keyword analysis to backlink evaluation, these tools can help you stay ahead of SEO trends.

## Tools:

1. **Text generators:** ChatGPT, Jasper, Copy.ai, Anyword, Sudowrite, Quillbot, Hivemind, Writesonic, WordAi, Rytr, Lumar, Magic write, Byword, Hubspot, Scalenut, Neuraltex, Notion AI, Mem, Frase, Writer, Wordtune, Hyperwrite, Chibi, ParagraphAI, Copymatic, Simplified, GrowthBar, GrammarlyGO, Surfer, Copysmith, Longshot, Hypotenuse AI, INK, Smart Copy, Outranking, StoryLab.ai, Wordtune,

2. **Image generators:** Dalle 2, Midjourney, Leonardo, Playground, Canva, Dream Studio, Picsart, BING Image Generator, Jasper Art, Starry AI, Dream by Wombo, Nightcafe, Synthesys X, Deep Dream Generator, Deep AI, Fotor, Craiyon, Artbreeder, Photosonic, Big Sleep, Freepik AI image generator, Stable Diffusion Online

3. **Video generators & editors:** Pictory, Veed.io, Synthesys, Synthesia, InVideo, DeepbrainAI, Elai.io, HeyGen, Colossyan, Synths Video, FlexClip, Wave Video, GliaCloud, Lumen5, Designs.ai, Wisecut, Runway, RawShorts, YouCam Video, Magisto, Adobe Premiere Pro, CapCut,

4. **Other SEO tools:** AlliAI, SEO AI, Pro Rank Tracker, Surfer SEO, SEM Rush, Ahrefs, Ubersuggest, Google Keyword Planner, Senuto, Diib, CanIRank, Market Muse, Wordlift, Nitropack, PageSpeed Insights, SE Ranking, SpyFu, WooRank, Seobility, Raven Tools, Conductor, Sistrix,

So there you have it! With ChatGPT and many other AI tools, you're not just leveraging AI in your SEO strategy – you're embracing the future. Remember, SEO is a marathon, not a sprint. And with your new AI buddies, you're going to do great! Keep going, and happy optimizing!

## 9.3. How to Keep Websites SEO Compliant Over Time?

Hi again! By now, you're becoming quite the SEO expert. But, as you've probably realized, SEO isn't a set-it-and-forget-it kind of thing. It's more like a garden that needs regular tending to keep growing and blooming. So, let's talk about how to keep your website SEO compliant over time.

**1. Regularly Update Your Content:** Like a fresh apple pie, content is best when it's fresh out of the oven. Keep your content up-to-date and relevant, and don't be afraid to update old posts with new information.

**2. Keep an Eye on Your Backlinks:** Backlinks are like thumbs-up from other websites, but not all thumbs-up are equal. Regularly check your backlink profile to ensure you're getting quality links and disavow any spammy or low-quality ones.

**3. Regular Technical SEO Checks:** Regularly check on key technical SEO aspects like page load speed, mobile-friendliness, and broken links. Tools like Google Search Console can be a big help here.

**4. Stay On Top of Algorithm Updates:** Google's algorithm changes more often than fashion trends. Stay informed about these updates as they can impact your SEO strategy.

**5. Monitor Your SEO Metrics:** Keep a close eye on your key SEO metrics like organic traffic, bounce rate, and conversion rate. These can give you insights into what's working and what needs tweaking.

**6. Regular Keyword Research:** Just like trends, popular keywords can change over time. Regular keyword research can help you stay on top of what your audience is currently interested in.

**7. Competitor Analysis:** Keep your friends close and your competitors closer! Regularly analyze your competitors' strategies to see what they're doing well and where you can outperform them.

**8. User Experience:** Always strive to improve user experience on your website. Remember, a happy user is more likely to become a loyal customer.

**9. Mobile Optimization:** With more than half of all web traffic coming from mobile devices, it's crucial to ensure your website is mobile-friendly. Regularly test your website on different devices and screen sizes to ensure a smooth user experience for all.

**10. Regular Audits:** Schedule regular SEO audits to analyze your website's current standing. This can help you identify what's working, what's not, and where there's room for improvement.

**11. Engage with Your Audience:** Respond to comments on your blog posts and social media channels. This not only boosts user engagement but also signals to search engines that your website is active and valuable to visitors.

**12. Keep Your Website Secure:** Security is a key aspect of user experience. Ensure your site is HTTPS and keep your site's security measures up to date to protect your visitors' information.

**13. Update Your Local SEO:** If you're a local business, keep your local listings and Google My Business profile up-to-date. This includes updating your opening hours, adding photos, and responding to reviews.

**14. Optimize Your Images:** Regularly check that all your images are properly formatted and have descriptive alt text. This not only helps with site speed but also makes your site more accessible.

**15. Follow Webmaster Guidelines:** Google's Webmaster Guidelines provide best practices to help Google find, crawl, and index your site. Make sure to follow these guidelines and regularly check for any updates.

Remember, SEO is an ongoing journey, not a destination. By continually monitoring and updating your website, you'll ensure it stays SEO compliant and keeps delivering the results you want. Keep rocking the SEO world!

## Let's test yourself!

**1. If SEO were a garden, which of these activities would NOT be part of your regular gardening routine?**

a) Planting fresh content like they're sunflower seeds.

b) Ignoring all the spammy weeds (backlinks) that pop up.

c) Taking out your technical SEO toolkit to fix broken links.

d) Keeping an eye out for any new Google-birds (algorithm updates) visiting your garden.

**2. Why is mobile optimization as important as choosing the right emoji for your text message?**

a) Because Google thinks it's cool.

b) Because more than half of all web traffic comes from mobile devices.

c) Because it's a fun challenge to make your website look good on a tiny screen.

d) Because your cat told you so.

**3. In the world of SEO, what does staying "fashion-forward" mean?**

a) Wearing the latest designer clothes while you update your website.

b) Staying updated with the latest memes to use in your content.

c) Keeping on top of the latest algorithm updates.

d) Making sure your website looks good in all the latest web browsers.

**4. If your website were a rock band, why would regular SEO reviews and updates be like your rehearsals?**

a) Because they're a necessary evil.

b) Because they help you keep your performance (SEO metrics) in check.

c) Because they're a good excuse to hang out with your bandmates (website visitors).

d) Because they give you a chance to play your favorite songs (keywords) over and over.

Remember to check the answers at the end of the book!

# 10.  Conclusion

## 10.1. Key Points to Remember

1. **SEO is Like Baking a Cake:** Just like how a cake needs the right ingredients, SEO needs a mix of the right strategies. From keywords, meta tags, to mobile-friendly designs and fast page load speeds, each ingredient contributes to the deliciousness of your website.

2. **Patience is a Virtue:** SEO is not an instant process; it's like planting a seed and waiting for a tree to grow. It takes time to see the fruits of your labor, but when you do, it's totally worth the wait. Remember, Rome wasn't built in a day, and neither are top-ranking websites.

3. **Content is King:** The foundation of your SEO is high-quality, engaging content. Focus on creating content that provides value to your readers. Include relevant keywords naturally and remember, write for humans first, search engines second!

4. **Link Building is Networking:** Building high-quality backlinks is like building a network in the real world. It's about creating relationships and providing value. And remember, like any good

relationship, quality matters more than quantity.

5. **Data is Your Compass:** Tools like Google Analytics are your guide in the SEO journey. They help you understand where you're going right and where you might need a course correction. So, learn to interpret the data and let it guide your SEO strategies.

6. **SEO is Always Changing:** SEO is a dynamic field with regular updates and changes. Staying updated on the latest trends and algorithm changes is crucial to staying ahead of the game.

7. **Don't Neglect Technical SEO:** Ensuring your website is technically sound, with fast page load speed, clean code, proper use of robots.txt file, a well-structured XML sitemap, and secure HTTPS protocol is as important as the content on your website.

8. **Mobile-First is a Must:** With more and more people browsing the web on their mobile devices, having a mobile-friendly website is no longer optional, it's a necessity. Make sure your site looks and functions great on all screen sizes to provide the best user experience possible.

9. **Local SEO is a Game-Changer:** If you're a local business, focusing on local SEO can help you stand out in your area. Optimize your Google

My Business listing, use local keywords, and collect positive reviews to improve your visibility in local search results.

10. **User Experience is Paramount:** At the end of the day, the main goal of SEO is to provide a better user experience. Google's algorithms aim to promote the most relevant and user-friendly pages. So, make sure your site is easy to navigate, content is easy to read, and users can find what they're looking for quickly and easily. If your users are happy, search engines will be too!

Remember, SEO isn't just about pleasing search engines – it's about making your website better for the people who visit it. Keep your users at the forefront of your SEO strategy, and you'll be on the right track.

## 10.2. Next Steps in Learning SEO

1. **Keep Learning:** SEO is a vast field that's constantly evolving. What works today may not

work tomorrow. Therefore, continuous learning is essential. There are many online resources, courses, blogs, and forums where you can expand your knowledge. Websites like Moz, Search Engine Journal, and of course, Google's own SEO guide, are excellent places to start.

2. **Get Hands-On:** There's nothing like getting your hands dirty to really understand SEO. Theory is great, but practice is where the magic happens. Try optimizing a website and monitor the results. Make changes, experiment, and learn from your successes and failures.

3. **Stay Updated:** Google and other search engines frequently update their algorithms. These changes can sometimes have a significant impact on SEO strategies. Following SEO news websites, subscribing to SEO newsletters, and participating in SEO communities can help you stay on top of these updates.

4. **Explore Tools:** There are plenty of SEO tools out there that can make your job easier. From keyword research tools like SEMRush and Ahrefs, to analytics tools like Google Analytics, there's a tool for almost every aspect of SEO. Get to know them and understand how they can help you.

5. **Attend Webinars/Workshops:** Many industry experts conduct webinars and workshops. These can be great opportunities to learn new strategies and stay abreast of the latest developments in the field. Plus, they often offer the chance to ask questions and interact with other SEO enthusiasts.

6. **Patience is Key:** SEO isn't a sprint; it's a marathon. Results often take time. Don't get discouraged if you don't see immediate improvements. Stay patient, keep optimizing, and results will come.

7. **Never Stop Optimizing:** SEO is an ongoing process. Even when you've achieved your initial goals, there's always room for improvement. Whether it's finding new keywords, improving page load times, or creating fresh content, there's always something to be done.

8. **Learn from Others:** Join SEO forums and communities. Engage with other SEO enthusiasts and professionals. You'll be surprised how much you can learn from the experiences of others.

With these steps, you're well on your way to becoming an SEO whiz. Remember, the journey of a thousand miles begins with a single step. So, put on your SEO shoes and start your journey. Happy optimizing!

# Let's test yourself!

**1. Which of the following is NOT a key point to remember about SEO?**

a) SEO is a one-time thing

b) SEO is a marathon, not a sprint

c) User Experience is paramount

d) Content is king

**2. What should you do to keep up with the ever-changing landscape of SEO?**

a) Ignore all the changes and stick to the basics

b) Keep learning and stay updated

c) Only follow the changes in Google's algorithm

d) Rely solely on SEO tools

**3. In your next steps of learning SEO, why is it important to get hands-on experience?**

a) Because theory is boring

b) It's not important at all

c) To see the impact of changes you make and learn from real scenarios

d) Because your hands feel left out

## 4. What does "Content is King" mean in the world of SEO?

a) You should have a king write your content

b) Only content about kings performs well in SEO

c) Content is only important for the game of chess

d) High-quality, relevant content is crucial in SEO

Check your answers at the end of the book!

# The Friendly Farewell: Your SEO Journey Continues

We've journeyed together from the basic understanding of what SEO is, through the nooks and crannies of keyword research, content optimization, technical SEO, and all the way to interpreting data and staying up-to-date with the ever-evolving landscape of SEO.

If there's one thing to remember from this guide, it's that SEO is not a one-time thing but a continuous process. It's a marathon, not a sprint. It's about learning, adapting, and growing with the ebbs and flows of search engine algorithms and user behavior.

As you close this guide, remember that you're not closing your journey with SEO. In fact, you're just getting started. SEO, like any other skill, gets better with practice. So, don't be afraid to dive in, get your hands dirty, and learn from real-life experiences.

We hope you found this guide useful, informative, and enjoyable. We've tried to make SEO as friendly and approachable as possible because we believe that everyone - yes, including you - can master it!

Remember, the world of SEO is as vast as it is fascinating, and there's always more to learn. So keep reading, keep exploring, keep experimenting, and keep growing.

Thank you for embarking on this SEO adventure with us. We can't wait to see where your SEO journey takes you next. Keep reaching for the stars!

## Tests' answers:

**Chapter 1:** 1.C, 2.B, 3.C, 4.D, 5.D

**Chapter 2:** 1.C, 2.B, 3.C, 4.C, 5.B

**Chapter 3:** 1.C, 2.B, 3.C, 4.A, 5.C

**Chapter 4**: 1.B, 2.B, 3.C, 4.C, 5.C, 6.B, 7.C, 8.B, 9.B, 10.B

**Chapter 5.** 1.C, 2.B, 3.C, 4.C, 5.A

**Chapter 6.** 1.C, 2.C, 3.C, 4.C, 5.C

**Chapter 7.** 1.B, 2.D, 3.D, 4.B, 5.B, 6.B, 7.C, 8.B, 9.A

**Chapter 8.** 1.C, 2.C, 3.C, 4.C, 5.B

**Chapter 9.** 1.B, 2.B, 3.C, 4.B

**Chapter 10.** 1.A, 2.B, 3.C, 4.D

www.ingramcontent.com/pod-product-compliance
Lightning Source LLC
La Vergne TN
LVHW051655050326
832903LV00032B/3819